MICHAEL C. GADWAY

YOU'RE WITH ME NOW

*Lessons From God and Roy Eugene Davis,
A Self-Realized American Yoga Master*

Copyright © 2024, Rev. Michael C. Gadway
All Rights Reserved.
Holy Fig Tree Publications, Raleigh, NC
ISBN-13: 978-0-9985465-7-5

Contents

Dear Reader..4

The Great Aloneness..7

See the Light and Hear the call..13

Walk the Path of God...23

A Shift in Our Spiritual Paradigm...33

The Dissolution of Ego...43

The Patterns of Our Lives..51

In This World and the Next..57

The Last Years and Final Goodbye..61

MICHAEL C. GADWAY

Dear Reader,

It is a rare and precious gift of Spirit to be able to spend time, as they say in India, "At the feet of an enlightened master." I had that remarkable opportunity when I met and became a lifelong disciple of Roy Eugene Davis in 1988.

By the time I met him, he had already been teaching and ministering for over thirty years, and he was respected as a spiritual authority the world over. He had traveled extensively for nearly sixteen years, and finally settled down in Lakemont, Georgia at the Center for Spiritual Awareness in 1972; though he continued to travel and teach right up to the end of his life. He was a prolific writer with over 50 published books, a dozen or so courses, and thousands of articles to his credit. He was spiritual friends with awakened Souls from many traditions and his contemporaries such as great teachers like Swami Rama, Joel Goldsmith, and Swami Muktananda considered him an authentic spiritual light.

It was obvious to others and me he had a personal and mystical relationship with God. He expressed spiritual principles and concepts in ways that revealed his profound realization of Spirit. His wisdom was unassailable, his intelligence profound, and his accomplishments impressive. Yet, my observation was that he was a humble and quiet man, and he treated everyone with the respect that comes with knowing the truth about each person's divine essence.

A Guru's responsibility is more than just teaching. A Guru shares his or her consciousness with the willing and prepared disciple. A Guru knows the world, and our experiences in it are not a reflection of our hopes, dreams, and wishes, nor are they a reflection of our consciousness. The world expresses as fulfilled or unfulfilled, as more or less, as joyous or miserable, according to what we can contain within our consciousness. A Guru knows if we want our world to change, our consciousness must expand to contain the change, with its new paradigm, within us. The bigger the consciousness vessel, the more Spirit can fill it. Then and only then, will our experience of the world shift, because it is true, 'As within so without.'

Roy Eugene Davis was one such enlightened Soul. To be in his presence was consciousness transforming and life altering. The power of God flowed from him and blessed those seeking spiritual refuge. When I was with him my troubles faded, my mind cleared, and the wondrous possibilities inherent to Spirit opened, and my consciousness expanded to contain them. My life improved with understanding and realization when I surrendered to the omnipresent Spirit that poured from him, and as him. I learned to make better choices from him and how to live a responsible, dharmic life.

I wish I could express my gratitude for him in words that would reflect the personal depth of change he engendered. My Guru was the cornerstone in my search for self-actualization and Self-realization. His support and encouragement gave rise to a bravery and fortitude I never believed were within me or possible. His training and his example have served me well to this day. He was a beacon of spiritual light shining through the darkness of delusion, and I will be eternally grateful.

...Jai Sat Guru

MICHAEL C. GADWAY

Chapter 1

The Great Aloneness
Endless space with infinite potential

We all have our stories; some stories are tales of wonderment and triumph with grand accomplishments and the rewards of acknowledgement and success. From these joyous dream stories arise the philosophies that tell us we are supported by a nurturing and caring universal God in this short sojourn we call life.

These philosophies tell us that if we can visualize with belief and feeling, all we righteously desire we can attain. Because after all, we are worthy as spiritual beings to have everything we need and want effortlessly provided. We are rays of the one light and therefore all that the light contains within it, we too contain within us; entire spiritual movements are based in this belief.

But other dream stories are sad to tell; they are filled with loss and sorrow, chocked full of emptiness and failure. These dream experiences are more akin to nightmares. From these stories arise the philosophies of detachment, surrender, and radical acceptance.

These philosophies tell us that life is a delusion and we must learn to see through it and beyond it, to the reality that lies behind it. We are not meant to get caught in this silky web we call life and that any manipulation of universal mind further ensnares us in ego. We are destined to transcend this dream by awakening from this world and learning to navigate it free from desires. These philosophies lead us to the understanding that suffering is inherent to all life in the material realm, but that there is a way out through detachment and enlightenment.

But life isn't black and white, nor are its spiritual and religious philosophies. Even when great saints and seers transcend the mind, and this mundane realm, and experience absolute existence-being, they must return and express this experience and their realizations through the limited mind with all its social, cultural, and intellectual shadings. I understand there is a supportive spiritual energetic, and we can learn to cooperate with it. But it is not a supernal giving tree just waiting for us to pluck its fruit to satisfy our yearnings. This force that some refer to as 'Grace', does not care if we have what we want or desire. It moves undeterred by our circumstance and understanding, towards the source and we can learn to move with it or we can resist it by trying to impose our individual will upon it and our world.

The more we try to carve out a place in this realm, the more we reinforce our sense of a separate self, and the further we move away from realization of our oneness with God. I know radical acceptance and surrender to the source is my path to freedom. But I am also acutely aware that each path is unique and my path is not for everyone. It is up to the individual to find his or her own way.

Regardless of the personal philosophy we have developed from your own experiences this lifetime, and no matter how our story is unfolding, whether we are full of joy or overwhelmed with sadness, we must not let it prevent us from finding God and freedom.

There is one thing spiritual aspirants of every enlightenment tradition learn to do; we learn to include the Divine in our daily life. We include God in our moments of joy, our moments of sadness, our quiet moments, and our active ones. We make God part of our story: including God in our lives excludes hopelessness from our lives.

If we include God in our story, over time, our story becomes the pursuit of God. We go from keeping our appointment with God, through prayer and meditation, to living, breathing, and moving in God no matter our story. We go from thinking about God to realizing God is expressing as us and through us. We develop and nurture a mystical relationship with the Divine when we unremittingly include God in everything we think and do. Then our story moves from searching for freedom to living in freedom. The more we include God, the more we see through the dream to the wonderous Reality behind it.

I don't remember a time when I wasn't looking for God. My relationship with God began early this lifetime, and my death heralded an end to my involvement with the Catholic church and a rebirth into a more profound spirituality. My parents were born and raised in a small resort town in the mountains of upstate New York where they chose to stay and raise a family. They were small business entrepreneurs and invested in a motel which they ran as a family business. When I was four years old, I spent my days by my mother's side as she watched and managed the front desk. She had her hands full with the business and I was a rambunctious child, full of an energy that was uncontainable.

Spring had come to the mountains and the temperature had risen above freezing. While snow was still on the ground and icicles hung from the eaves, they were melting as the sun shone brightly in the sky on a background of cloudless blue. Desperate to play in the sun, I began to harangue my mother to let me go outside and play. I wouldn't take no for an answer and finally, worn down from my pleading, she said, "Okay." She dressed me in warm clothes and instructed me to stay on the front steps where she could keep an eye on me. I happily agreed as I put the leash on our dog and bounded out the door. The phone rang just then, and my mother answered it, looking away for just a few minutes. She looked back to find me gone and quickly put on her coat and went looking for me. When she got outside, she looked down to see my tracks in the snow leading towards the far end of the motel where the pool was located. She followed my footprints, and when she got to the pool, she found me face down in the water, under the ice, deprived of oxygen, completely blue. She pulled my lifeless body from the water, wrapped me in her coat, and ran with me in her arms to the front desk. She called 911 and began to give me mouth to mouth recusation.

The ambulance came and brought me to the hospital Emergency Room. A priest had been called, and while the doctor tried to revive my body, he administered last rights. But the doctor was unable to revive me and walked into the waiting room to tell my parents he hadn't been able to save me. At that moment, our family doctor, who had been called by my father, bound into the room. Exclaiming "Bullshit," he ran into the Emergency Room. There, he started my heart back up and was able to bring me back to this world. He kept a "Little Red Book of Miracles," a list of the people whose lives he saved. I was his first entry in the book. I lay sleeping, near coma, for three days. My family took shifts by my bedside. On the third day, I woke, and turning to my French Catholic Aunt Margaret I said, "I've seen God." She went to Mass every day for the rest of her life after that.

I don't remember seeing a personal God, but I do remember the experience. I was floating in a place of profound stillness and indescribable peace. A place of endless space and infinite potential. That place the Buddhists call the "void," and Yoga refers to as Kaivalya, The Great Aloneness.

While I was sleeping, the medical staff put IVs in both my wrists and ankles. Thrashing in my sleep, I tore them out requiring stiches in all four limbs. To this day I have scars in the form of the cross on both my ankles and wrists. A reminder that my days as a Catholic are over, and I have a new life born of water and Spirit.

God has always been with me through the difficult periods of my life. Whenever life threatened to overwhelm me, Spirit rushed in to grace me with uplifting and sacred events. The home I grew up in was a familial war zone. I was the target of an abusive triangulation and the victim of mental, emotional, verbal, and physical abuse. Along with the abuse at home, I was being sexually abused outside the home. At the age of ten, the abuse escalated on both fronts, and I sank into a dazed confusion.
Unable to find a safe place either at home or school, I would seek out places of solitude where I was out of harm's way. To this day, I need to spend long periods of aloneness to recharge and rest.

The extreme abuse lasted nearly three years and during this period of my life, my Soul took flight searching for refuge in subtle realms. Often, I would awaken in the middle of the night in that place I earlier described as Kaivalya, drifting effortlessly in that 'Peace which surpasses understanding.' I would return to the body hours later. When I did, the body would often be corpse like, without feeling, numb, and heavy. Sometimes, I would return to the body and my sight or hearing would be gone. During those occasions, I would make my way out to the den and sit on a chair alone in the middle of the night waiting for them to return. I never panicked or cried out, something inside seemed to know that this was natural. Within ten to twenty minutes of sitting quietly, my senses would return to normal, and I returned to bed. For three years this was a regular occurrence and I felt comforted and found peace in the spiritual experiences I later came to know as Samadhis. Looking back all these years later, I'm sure these supernal awakenings in the dark nights of the Soul, were the gifts of grace and Spirit shining a light to save me. Without them, I shudder to think what I would have become.

I learned, from years of experience and with my Guru's blessing, that Spirit is in the suffering and pain in the same measure as It is in the joy and peace. It lies just beneath our thoughts and feelings regardless of their degree or intensity. This life is a dream play, a Lila. Sometimes the dream is light and joyful, and sometimes the dream is dark and painful. But it is still just a dream, a delusion.

I somehow made it through my childhood and teenage years, but not without emotional scars that took years to come to terms with, heal, and finally move beyond their reach. I had two more near death experiences but somehow survived it all. I left home at seventeen, put myself through college, and moved out into the workforce. But through those years, I had a deeply personal prayer life and there was never a day that went by that I didn't talk to God and ask for guidance.

Chapter 2

See the Light and Hear the Call

*The heart beats to an unstruck melody.
The mind stops to listen to the music.
The Soul dances in surrendered bliss
when the song is finally heard.*

There are profound moments in each of our spiritual journeys when God asks us to choose who we want to be and how we are going to live. In moments of such dramatic poignancy, time comes to a standstill, and the truth of who and what we are looks back at us from the mirror of introspection with a blunt and uncompromising glare; that timeless hour, that endless minute, that forever second, when the soundless reflection of our lives, staring back at us, compels us to ask, "Who am I, and what is my purpose?"

MICHAEL C. GADWAY

These are moments of awakening when the undeniable starkness of our current reality and the grayness of our everyday existence creates a Soul yearning for the light of freedom so strong, so overwhelming, we can only bow our heads, feeling the fullness of separation and suffering as it washes over us. Knowing it is impossible for us to return in consciousness to the way we were before, we begin our search for joy, peace, and lasting happiness.

All through my teen years and into my twenties, I looked for God, though I had no understanding of what that meant. I spent my days looking for God and myself, not realizing they were the same thing to be found in the same place. I first returned to the Catholic church, but soon realized it held no profound meaning for me. I then began searching through other Christian churches and even explored the Pentecostal movement. But, watching them thrash about and pretend to speak in tongues was off-putting to say the least. I then moved on to study Edgar Cayce, but found that equally dissatisfying. After that, I began to read New Age material with the same disenchantment. The whole time my heart called to God and I looked for salvation around every corner. I hungered for someone or something to show me God.

That dramatic awakening of consciousness I had been searching for, came during my twenty-sixth year. I was working for a regional company and I had been transferred to St. Simons Island, Georgia. To an outsider, my life would have seemed ideal; I was living on an island. I had a wife, and a new son. I was rising up the corporate ladder and everything appeared to be exactly what I wanted. But I was desperately unhappy inside at the deepest level, and I didn't understand why. I yearned for something more. I didn't realize at the time, but I was experiencing a kind of Divine discontent. I knew only that I felt empty, and hollow, and Soul crushingly lost.

Having a rare Tuesday off, I decided I needed some time alone. With my wife at work, I dropped my son off at day care and went for a run. While I was running, my heart began to ache, and I prayed "God, are you there? I need you." It was the only thought I had and it played over and over again. By the time I returned home, I was single mindedly engrossed in the prayer and my need for God to answer me. Walking into the den, with my head bent low, and my heart heavy, I fell to my knees and began to pray in earnest.

I cried out for God's intervention. As my desire for God grew more heated, sweat began to drip from every pore of my body. After a very long-time crying, and praying, finally exhausted and spent, the last thing I remember saying to God before I fell asleep on the floor was, "God, if you don't help me, I will not be here tomorrow." It wasn't a threat; it was a simple statement of fact. Then, I fell asleep on the floor where I lay.

I don't know how long I slept, but as I lay there, a great light blossomed from within, enfolding me and filling me to overflowing, growing in intensity until only light remained: no body, no mind, no me. Only light and joy, ebbing and flowing, pulsating and reverberating, like a pure white blissful sun. Slowly, as the experience began to fade, and I returned to body consciousness, a great peace settled upon me and sighing deeply, I fell back asleep. When I awoke again, the feelings of despair and hopelessness were gone and, in their place, there was only contentment and a knowing that everything was going to be alright.

It is in these moments, when our consciousness expands beyond its previous conceptual boundaries, that we are given the beautiful gift of God's grace and the awareness we can either choose to step into the current of Spirit leading us home, or turn and walk the other way. Often, we hesitate because we know if we step into the current and surrender, we are choosing to let it take us where it will. But the truth is, all choice distills to a single choice; will we surrender to God's will or continue to walk in the shadow of egoic delusion?

Our hearts greatly desire to surrender to the Infinite, but our minds resist. Indentured by the delusive hold of subliminal mental afflictions churning within us, we move through this life locked tightly in the grips of attachment, aversion, desire, fear, and doubt. We wander darkly the roads of sensuality and materialism, and night walk through our days unaware of the light of Spirit shining just beneath the surface of our awareness, unseen and unknown.

We, as Souls, intuitively understand grace and its redemptive role. We know there is a supportive and nurturing spiritual energy flowing through all creation and we can learn to participate with it. Grace is not the unknowable, untenable, etheric energy of an omnipresent, omnipotent being higher than us, capriciously deciding who to help and who not to help. Grace is the infallible divine intelligence in action, available to us all, and its presence is potently experienced when we surrender to the Infinite in whatever form we perceive it. Grace is witnessed in the compassion of others: by the hand reaching out to help us up when we stumble and fall, by the arms embracing us when we suffer, by the tears of another, shed for us when we are in pain, by the appearance of our spiritual teacher when we most need him or her.

Grace demonstrated its action in my life the day after I 'saw the light.' I had heard of a small meditation center on the island called the Center for Spiritual Awareness or CSA. But, when someone had mentioned it to me earlier, I dismissed it as another new age dead end. However, that day, I decided to call and see what they were about. The person on the phone was professional and kind. She invited me to come to meditation the next evening. I took down the address and thanked her, making up my mind to attend. The following night, when I sat for the first time in meditation with several other people in a small sanctuary, a sense of Spirit and destiny saturated the room. There before me were the pictures of the Gurus of the Kriya Yoga tradition. The last picture was of a dignified middle-aged man dressed in a coat and tie. I was later to learn his name was Roy Eugene Davis, the founder of CSA, headquartered in Lakemont, GA. As I sat in the silence, I heard a sound ringing in my ears. It slowly grew in intensity until it alone was the only focus of my awareness. The sound seemed to have no beginning or end. It poured through me sending a shiver up my spine and pulling my awareness into the higher brain centers. It was the great OM, the pronouncement, the vibratory hum of the universe. A deep calm and a sense of belonging filled me. I knew I had found my spiritual home and without ever having met him, and knowing nothing about him, I knew Roy Eugene Davis was my Guru.

God often sends awakened Souls here to help us on our pilgrimage home. They are spiritual lighthouses, illuminating the darkness of ignorance and guiding us over the treacherous seas of delusion. My Guru, Roy Eugene Davis, was one such beacon of light, and his presence and God-realized consciousness was the single most important gift of grace I was ever to receive.

The first lesson I learned from Roy came as the answer to a question. I asked him, while visiting CSA the next summer, "When I die, will my Soul..." Before I had finished asking the question, he was shaking his head no. I stopped mid-sentence and looked at him. His gaze seemed to penetrate to the core when he slowly said, "You don't have a Soul, you are a Soul." The weight of his simple words and the depth of his consciousness had a profound effect on my psyche. I went silent, internalizing his realization as my own.

You see, we are living tributaries. Our individualized spiritual existence reflects and honors the Universal Spirit that is the heart of us all. God breathes, we are his breath. God cries, we are her tears. God sees, we are the living colors swirling in ever mystical beauty. We are the trees of his forest, the waves of her ocean, the rays of his sun. There can be no God without us, and there can be no us without God.

Somewhere, deep inside us, we know we are the weft threads of a seraphic tapestry: a blended miracle of spirit and light. But we also know we are more than just a product; we are the hand God put forth when woven is this world. We are the waters of life, and the life that moves those same waters. We are the actor and the play. We are the witness and the drama. We are not born, and we will not die; we live in the forever realm of Spirit because we are that same Spirit made manifest.

God is the truth of us. God is the heart of us. God is the journey and the destination. We have not been left abandoned in the cold to find our way home alone. We have only to turn to the source within, that consciousness-presence silently waiting to be called upon. But, to realize this truth, we need to learn to intently listen to the song of our Soul. And to do this, everything we are not must come to a complete, absolute, and unconditional stop. Our bodies must still, our thoughts must recede, our in-breath must surrender to our out-breath. It is then we step outside the boundary of time to experience the truth of our existence-being. It is then, time ceases to exist for us because for time to exist, there must be motion, and without motion this time-space continuum has no relevance to us or reality for us. We step into breathless, timeless, eternity when it all grinds to a halt.

In this infinite, timeless moment, we realize the truth of our spiritual existence, and we are never the same again. The bliss of our being soars broad without the constraints of self-doubt and unworthiness. We rise, higher and higher, on the winds of God consciousness, weightless, having shed all fear, desire, attachment, and aversion.

Our common journey is in the pursuit of perfection, realized in the transfixion of Spirit; this perfection in stillness is achieved by the acceptance and transcendence of our human imperfection. Our sojourn comes to an end when we radically accept, and then leave behind the false belief that we are separate and unworthy of unity with the creator of all things.

We are on a pilgrimage to wholeness whether we realize it or not. Aspiring to completeness and oneness is yearning for perfection. Built into our Soul destiny, by that same divine intelligence running the universe, is the Soul's hunger to reunite with the Source. It is a pilgrimage to the temple of the greater Self, the Spirit, that fountain dwelling within. It is only our resistance to this divine intelligence that keeps us in bondage. We resist our thoughts. We resist our circumstances. We resist the path laid at our feet. We resist the table Spirit has prepared for us. In this resistance we squander our resources, our time, and our life energy. Resistance to the flow of Spirit is often expressed in the form of ego trying to make things happen in this life. We resist the timing of Spirit and begin to enforce our own agenda; we push too hard. We plan too much and attempt to control this life and our circumstances. To find God, we must surrender to the Infinite with clear minds and open hearts. The divine intelligence running the universe has a perfect time table awaiting us if only we open ourselves to it and follow its lead.

Within just a few weeks of attending meditations on the island, I began to yearn to go to CSA and meet the man I was sure was my Guru. The desire grew stronger as the days passed. Finally, the hunger grew so strong I decided to leave home the next week and pilgrimage to CSA. The only thing left to do was to tell work and my wife I was taking a week off which would have raised eyebrows since it was January and I had no vacation time left for the next 6 months. But still, I went to sleep that night sure I had made the right decision and determined to tell them the next day.

Sometime around 3:00 AM, I was stirred awake by a gentle breeze sweeping across my face. Opening my eyes, I saw Roy standing at the foot of my bed smiling at me. His body seemed to be made of light and color. He looked at me with deep brown eyes and I heard his voice in my head say, "Wait until the summer to come." Then he vanished. I sat straight up in bed, wanting to make sure it wasn't a dream. Sitting in the dark silence of the night for several minutes, processing what had just happened, I waited until I was again calm to lay back down and try to go to sleep. But sleep did not come easily, and what sleep I got was filled with thoughts of my Guru.

Shortly after Roy's astral visit, I was transferred to Raleigh NC. I went ahead of my family and stayed in a motel while looking for a place for us to live. It was during that interlude, just before my family moved to be with me, that I had a superconscious experience that shifted my entire spiritual paradigm. After it, I never saw the world in the same way again. One night, after work, I sat to meditate on the motel bed. As I looked deeply into the third eye, I suddenly felt Roy's presence. His spirit saturated the room and a hushed sacredness descended on me. Then, my consciousness seemed to expand beyond its boundaries. It burst open and within it the entire material realm seemed to be floating. I witnessed swirling spirals of stars and nebulas. Whole galaxies collided with new planets and new suns being formed and destroyed. Lights and colors amassed and dispersed. All creation seemed to be spiraling out from a central point of great stillness. As I watched, all this and more, I was drawn into that single point of consciousness as if a great force called me home. There, any sense of individuality vanished. It was no longer God and me. There was only Spirit and an endless overflowing fountain of bliss. When I finally opened my eyes, it was late into the night. I lay down and slept till dawn.

There is a myth perpetuated by many spiritual teachers and communities from previous generations. They claim we must earn our freedom from suffering through atonement and penance, and that it may take lifetimes to do this. But we do not suffer because we have sinned or strayed from the path. We suffer because we have forgotten the truth and the truth is remembered and realized by simply waking up. There is no ransom, no punishment from God awaiting us. The only blockades are those of self-doubt and self-hatred. The only restrictions preventing our realization of our eternal truth are to be found in the mind: those of attachment, aversion, desire, fear, and loathing. If we remove these mental clouds, the Soul-sun we are, illuminates the darkness of our ignorance and brings with it Divine remembrance. The light of our being is then seen and felt by the whole world and evidenced by the flawless action of grace leading us moment-to-moment.

We don't have to earn our freedom, we have only to turn inward and accept it as our own. We don't have to beg or pray, or claim anything from the Source because it is not being withheld from us. As we awaken, we begin to comprehend more and more the fullness of life and the endless supply the Source cannot help but provide to us, for us, and as us. We are Souls interacting with the world through these bodies and minds; we are individualized immortals of pure Spirit. We are made of God stuff. Our humanity, that essence common to us all, is that at our core, at the heart of us, we are spiritual beings having a communal dream we call life. We need only to awaken from the dream and that awakening begins in the heart.

MICHAEL C. GADWAY

Chapter 3

Walk the Path of God
*Hard fought and arduous won, whereon
the spiritual ground we stand resolute*

The way of the surrendered and open heart is committing to the journey even when the path we will tread is unknown. It is a pilgrimage of faith. But it is not faith in a God unfamiliar and outside ourselves. It is believing in the small, quiet voice of the consciousness-presence within us and letting it lead the way. The heart can hear this call best because it isn't bound by the confines of the mind. The mind, full of bias, trained limitations, and false beliefs, will decry aloud the possibility of freedom. But, when we can no longer bear the constraints of the mind, or stand to breathe the poison air of our self-made prisons, there comes upon us the willingness to step forth into the great spiritual unknown. We feel anything other than what we are currently experiencing must be better, higher, surer. The, as of yet, unrevealed path of Spirit becomes more real to us and we know we have no choice but to be true to ourselves and surrender to the Spirit within.

If there is a price to be paid to find God and dwell in the freedom of Soul-knowing, it is that the heart must open to experience unconditional love, and sometimes the heart must break or even shatter to open. The road to illumination is paved with cobblestones from our fractured egos. To open the heart, the ego, and all the imperfections that go with it, must be first radically accepted, then resolved, and finally dissolved into the emptiness of stillness; we learn to see the nothingness of our mental restrictions. This contemplative process requires the silence of seclusion. We must spend time alone in the quiet, dissolving the mental restrictions for the mind to become as pure as the Soul wielding it. It is only through the dissolution of the small self we realize the completeness and wholeness of our unity with the Universe.

The journey to completeness and wholeness begins and ends in the heart. The heart is the doorway to higher spiritual perceptions and it can only be opened with love and surrender. The heart is the gateway to peace, bliss, and freedom. When we throw open our hearts, we unlock the portal to Spirit and the sacred wonders that come with it. The heart is the entrance to true and profound acceptance. It is there the core of us is found and universal Spirit is realized; the heart reveals the truth of us.

God waits for us just behind the beating heart. Our spiritual journey through this world begins with the first heartbeat and ends with the last. If we are to be free, we must be brave; we need courage to be kind, compassionate, and loving. These are the traits of a true spiritual warrior. It takes strength to have a generous spirit in the face of hatred, bigotry, and misunderstanding. Kindness is the intrepid action of the spiritual seeker. Patience and determination are the silent virtues of those who would know God. Letting the heart lead, despite the protests of the mind, is the sign of an awakening Soul.

A steady and strong heart is required to walk the path that ascends the heights of spiritual realization. The higher we climb, the thinner the air and the fewer the travelers. But if we steadily carry on, relentless, undeterred by the challenges, altitude, and lack of companionship, one day we rise above the clouds and step into the clear blue sky of Spirit. Once we are committed to the awakening path, and surrendered to the process, the divine intelligence, inherent in life, shows us the righteous road meant only for us. If we are prepared, God sends us a guide who sees clearly our road to enlightenment. But often these teachers will test us to ensure we are committed to the path and all the challenges that come with walking it.

Knowing Roy Eugene Davis was my Guru, I planned a week the next summer to come to meet him. I arrived on Father's Day, 1988 in Lakemont, Georgia. As I turned off the highway onto the road leading to the retreat center, I rounded a curve with a slight incline, when suddenly it seemed as if all the air was sucked out of the car. I found myself in what Yogis refer to as "A windless spot." Just as I had the thought "What the..." I looked up to see Roy Eugene Davis drive slowly by me. Time stood still and he seemed to be driving in slow motion. The moment is etched in my memory and even today, decades later, when I think about it, I am transported to that moment and all that came with it. It was the igniting of a Guru-Disciple relationship that transcends time and space. Roy always seemed to be walking in what the Yoga Sutras refer to as a "dharmic cloud." In his presence I naturally became quiet and introspective. His consciousness was so attuned to the Infinite that when I was near him, I too felt closer to God. The next morning, I found myself sitting in the meditation hall, meditating with a Self-realized yoga master and the experience was transforming.

So sure was I, that Roy was my Guru, on Wednesday afternoon, I boldly walked up to his chalet where he worked and banged loudly on the glass door. Roy came to the door and when he answered, I asked him if we could talk. Nodding his head, we sat down together. He carried on some small talk, patiently waiting for me to get to the point. Without preamble, I blurted out, "Will you accept me for discipleship?" Caught off guard, he looked at me, paused, and said "No." I felt my heart sink and fold in on itself like so much wet cardboard. Then, he said, "Let's get to know each other first. You come back and we'll discuss it next year." He then went on to talk more but, honestly, I was so disappointed and my heart so dampened, I have no memory of what he said. When we parted, feeling immensely sorry for myself, I went behind the Yoga Dome to be alone. Depressed and saddened by what I perceived as rejection, I sat stewing in my melancholy when something inside of me shifted and I became resolute. I said to myself, "I don't care how long it takes or how often I have to come back, he will accept me as his disciple."

Above the storms and beyond the noise of confusion, doubt, and suffering, we can rise to heights only imagined by dreamers and philosophers. If only we refuse to abandon our quest for the Infinite no matter the hurdles, and no matter how long it takes, we, the devotees of God, must never give up hope and faith. We need keep them close to our hearts, secret and safe, for these are our true travel companions and they will serve us well. I have read from unenlightened people that we need to give up hope to be happy.

But this is not so; we need let go of expectations, but that is not the same as hope. Hope and faith are the beacons that light our way to God despite the dark skies roiling over our heads or the storms ripping through our lives.

Often family and friends will challenge our thinking, inviting us to question and doubt ourselves, or feel like there is something wrong with us for choosing a path they don't approve of, or understand. Sometimes, as in my life, they become openly hostile when they are forced to face their own broken expectations, fears, and prejudices. But doubt and fear are terrible reasons not to do something profoundly life changing, just as guilt and shame are equally terrible reasons to stagnate under other's expectations. I was determined to do whatever it took to find God. I learned early on that no one can do for us that which we must do for ourselves, and I truly believe we come into this world with everything we need for our journey home. I have always known the difference between duty and dharma; duty is what the world tells us we should do. Dharma is what our hearts tell us we are meant to do. I knew I was meant to meet Roy, just as I knew I was meant to search for God and would never give up that search.

During my first summer with Roy at CSA, he addressed the challenges I was experiencing with my family and friends who didn't understand the choices I was making; it was Roy's custom, in those days, to go around the room and have the retreat participants share their names and where they lived. He seemed to enjoy hearing where everyone came from and he would mentally note if there were several people from a particular area who might be interested in holding a Kriya Yoga seminar. When it came my turn, I said "Michael Gadway, Raleigh, NC." He looked at me and quietly asked, "What do your parents think of you coming?" I was twenty-six years old and without a good filter when I said, "Oh, they think I'm worshipping cows." He said, "Cows huh." I said, "Yes sir." He asked, "What is their affiliation?" I told him the fundamentalist organization they belonged to; he just remained quiet. Then I blurted out, "Well, I guess it's better than nothing." To which Roy, in his inimitable wisdom said, "Oh, I don't know about that." He then became very quiet and I felt a shift in consciousness. Leveling his gaze at me he said, "Well, they don't need to worry. You're with me now." That simple commitment cemented my determination to stay with him and I became unwavering in my loyalty and determination.

I came back to CSA to be with Roy several times over the next year. I came to every retreat, every open weekend, and Holy Season meditation. It put stress on my family life and my work life but for me, it was a priority like no other I had ever had. I hungered to find God and I knew I needed Roy Eugene Davis to accomplish it. I wasn't interested in having a personal relationship with him. I wasn't interested in having another friend. I didn't care about his personal or social life. I asked myself only one question about him. "Could he show me God?"

Being in his consciousness-presence was life altering. Many spiritual traditions speak of the effects that occur when time is spent in the presence of an enlightened teacher. There is a transmission of spiritual energy known as 'shaktipat,' or 'saktipata.' In the Christian tradition, this is known as "the quickening," or "the transmission of the Holy Spirit." Shaktipat awakens dormant energies in the devotee and can often stir the prana stored in the lower chakras, known as kundalini, to flow up the spine more dynamically. During the summer after I met Roy, I experienced this transfer of spiritual energy in a profound way. The experience came just after I went home, having spent that first week at CSA in Roy's presence. I was awakened in the middle of the night by energy flowing up my spine. It would start in the lower back and course up my spine into the higher brain centers. It felt like liquid electricity infused with joy and bliss. It started slowly in short bursts then grew to more dynamic flows. They became so strong at one point, my back arched until only my head and hips were left on the bed. When they ended nearly three hours later, I was left exhausted and fell back to sleep until the next morning. When I awoke, a great joy stirred within me, and I remained in a state of bliss for the next three days.

I continued to visit Roy and CSA that year as often as I could and when the next June arrived, I was determined to ask him for discipleship again. I cornered him in the Meditation Hall Monday morning before the 10 a.m. class. I said to him, "You said 'come back and we'll discuss discipleship next year,' I have been coming back for a whole year now. Will you accept me for discipleship?" He became very solemn and nodded saying "Yes." Then he said. "Let this Kriya initiation be a new beginning for you, a rebirth. Stay very quiet this week. Don't socialize, don't talk too much, pray and meditate more, and contemplate higher realities." I said, "Yes sir." He gently said "Alright." He patted me on the shoulder, turned me around, putting his arm over my shoulders, we walked together toward the front of the room.

That week, I did as he asked. I kept to myself mostly, not socializing, not talking, staying inwardly turned, with my thoughts and prayers directed to God. I meditated several times a day and ate meagerly. By the time Thursday morning's Kriya initiation came, I was very quiet inside and acutely introspective. As I had throughout the past year, I got in line to receive his Kriya blessing. But this time, as my turn came, and I stepped toward him, everything changed; it was as if I had stepped onto the palm of God's hand. Once again, I found myself perfectly still in a 'windless spot.' When I reached Roy, I instinctively bowed to him with my hands pressed together in prayer. He bowed back with hands pressed together. Then, he took my right hand in his left, and placed his right hand over my forehead. I closed my eyes and looked up into that space between the eyebrows. Sensing I was nervous, he gently rocked my head back and forth to induce relaxation. Then he pushed my head back. When he did, I looked deeply into my third eye and I was startled to see his brown eyes staring back at me. Suddenly his eyes seemed to drive into me going deeper and deeper, piercing layer after layer, and dragging me in with them. My mind silenced, my heart stilled, and timed vanished; I found myself inwardly standing in a space of indescribable, profundity. There looking back at me was... me. I remember having the thought "Oh, it's me the personality looking at me the Soul." Then I had the realization, "Aha, I am that!" The moment I had the Soul-realization, he took his hand away. I staggered slightly at the disconnect. He held my hand tightly until I regained my balance then he moved me forward through the line as if nothing had happened. From then on, every Kriya initiation from Roy was some version of this; each time I would have the realization "Oh yes, I remember, I am that." He would take his hand away and move onto the next participant.

Roy became my Guru and guide. A more than thirty-year spiritual relationship began, changing the course of my life. He was my spiritual mentor and spiritual friend. He was my confidant. He was the spiritual lighthouse that shone bright across the dark waters of delusion and suffering. His importance in my life cannot be overstated. He showed me God and in doing so, gave me the one and only thing I truly wanted.

Over the years, I watched dozens, if not hundreds of people come and go. Some, who came to CSA were 'Guru shopping and ashram hopping,' more interested in 'signs and miracles' than actual spiritual liberation. He was polite and kind to these people, but he was also not interested in developing relationships with them. Roy refused to pander to egotists and he could not be bought, bribed, or charmed. He had a sixth sense and knew when people were not sincere. But if you were sincere and came back, the spiritual rewards were beyond measure. He not only shared his teachings but more importantly, his consciousness. To spend time in his presence and to share in his consciousness was transforming in ways I cannot put into words.

To this day, I sometimes think "Imagine what I would have missed if I had not been relentless, if I had walked away, feeling hurt, ego bruised, and had taken no for his answer." On the spiritual path there are many obstacles we must face, but the most delusive barrier to Self-realization we must overcome, is the arrogance and narcissism of the ego telling us we are either not good enough, or we are too good, too proud, to walk the path of God.

MICHAEL C. GADWAY

Chapter 4

A Shift in Our Spiritual Paradigm
This life is full of colors unseen and dreams unrealized

So many of us spend our time dreaming about how we want life to be, we forget to live the life we have. We live our lives in the shadows of our thoughts and beliefs hiding from the light of the Soul. But I know a secret; the truth is, the life we are experiencing is not a reflection of our hopes, dreams, and wishes, nor was it ever meant to be. What we are experiencing, whether we perceive it as pleasant or unpleasant, happy or sad, fulfilling or unfulfilling, is a reflection of what our consciousness can contain, made manifest. Consciousness, in this sense, is our fundamental spiritual perception and understanding of our world and our place in it. It is an intricate blend of the patterns carved into our minds from previous behaviors and beliefs, as well as our habitual states of awareness and thoughts (cognitive biases), and the level to which we realize the truth of our spiritual existence-being. The spiritual paradigm within which we function is our consciousness, and it is our consciousness that is expressing as our current events and circumstances.

If the world is a reflection of what our consciousness can contain, not just our thinking patterns, then trying to force God or life or the Universe into a form that suits us, and we mistakenly believe will make us happy, by manipulating the mind will have little to no permanent effect. If we do get what we want, it won't last. It will play itself out on the life stage and when the mental energy or determination behind the manifestation ebbs or fades away, we will be left in the same place we began, with little to no spiritual awakening having occurred.

In order for us to permanently change our world and our experiences in it, we must have a dramatic shift in our spiritual consciousness-paradigm. Our consciousness is not fixed; it is fluid and expansive, and with Spirit as its foundation, it is without limitations and boundaries. The more established we are in the truth of our existence-being, the more the infinite potential of our spirit-life we will express. Roy, being a true Sat-guru, established in truth, demonstrated this to me as a reality one summer while I was on retreat at CSA. During one of his morning lectures, he was discussing the possibility of us becoming conscious dreamers and thereby learning to change our perception of the world as a fixed object. If we could learn to see the fluidity of our dream world, we could start to realize the fluidity of our waking world as well, with the possibility of a different outcome being within our consciousness. While he was explaining this, he suddenly stopped and asked, "How many of you dream in color?" Most of the retreat participants raised their hands. He then said, "Oh, well how many of you dream in black and white?" Myself and four or five others raised our hands. But the room was full by the time I had arrived that morning, and I had to sit on the floor to his far-right where he couldn't easily see me. Raising his right hand, waving slightly, he very nonchalantly said, "My blessing for coming is that from now on, you'll dream in color." He never looked at me though and I thought, "Aren't they lucky, I wish he had seen me." I soon forgot about it and went on about my day. But that night, while sleeping, I became aware of myself dreaming. In my dream I was standing just outside the Meditation Hall. Looking up, I saw the flagpole still there today. While looking at the flagpole, suddenly a flag of brilliant red snapped before my eyes and wrapped itself around the pole. Then a flag of blue snapped before my vision, then yellow, and so on through the visible spectrum. I looked around me and watched in amazement as the grass turned green and the woods turned hues of auburn and brown and red. Then all the colors began to swirl together into a whirlpool before exploding in my vision as I woke up. From that night forward my dreams have been in color. To this day I have black and white memories and dreams from before I met Roy, and color memories and dreams that came after I met him. My life, by comparison seemed dull and lifeless before my Guru, and full of wonder and color after I met him.

A shift in our spiritual paradigm may come suddenly and dramatically, but more likely it unfolds gradually after we have prepared our psyches for the experience. The way this is done is by doing the 'inner work.' The inner work spiritual aspirants are called to do is to clean up all the negative cognitive biases, as well as the subconscious patterns locked into our minds. Thoughts of themselves have no power until they have been spiritualized. If we want to see our world change, we must do the inner work necessary to purify and shift our consciousness into a new and expanded paradigm.

Simply trying to force our mental images onto the stage of the material world will not work without the realization of our spiritual identities behind them. Even Jesus was quoted in the New Testament as saying, "I can of mine own self do nothing," (John 5:30). It is consciousness that affects change, not mental gymnastics. It isn't the mind by itself that profoundly changes our experiences. The mind may change our perception of our world, but if we truly want to change our world, it is the power of our realization and the depth of our consciousness working through the mind that will permanently alter it. To make the righteous changes we need and desire, we must do the inner spiritual work that prepares us for the consciousness paradigm shift. When we work on changing and expanding our consciousness, the world and our experience of it must change and expand with it.

Most people trying to create or manifest a world of their own choosing are either deluded or egotistically bound in their false and misguided whirlpools of awareness. In yogic terms, these people are coming from the lower three chakras. Though they claim to be coming from a higher spiritual viewpoint, they are, in fact, trapped in the delusion of this material world. This is evidenced when we listen to them speak. We hear statements such as "I manifest what I want," or "I am a co-creator/co-manifester," or "I simply imagine what I want." What these statements have in common is the ego expressing itself in the form of a deluded "I." They are claiming a spiritual identity in order to fulfill their needs and desires in the material world, rather than owning the realization that there is a Divine intelligence providing without effort and manipulation when we awaken to it. When the false sense of a separate existence dominates the consciousness, it is a red flag pointing towards egoism and egotism. I once asked my Guru about how to proceed into the future after a dramatic life changing event. His advice was simple and direct he said, "Be Spirit led."

YOU'RE WITH ME NOW

There is a Universal intelligence built into the fabric of nature. This intelligence is intuitive and infallible. It is sometimes referred to as the Universal Buddhi or Cosmic Mind. It is quantumly entangled with all manifestation from the material world we live in, to the highest of spiritual realms. This intelligence is inherent to the smallest unit of matter, referred to in Vedic literature as prana. Prana is the subtlest form of energy from which all other forms of energy are derived. It is intelligent, omnipresent, and quantumly entangled; there is nothing in existence that is not guided by this unerring intelligence, and we can learn to participate and cooperate with it. The more awake we are to the truth of our existence-being, the more aware we become of this divine intelligence guiding and leading us for our highest good.

Roy could dynamically move and control prana at will, simply with intent. I experienced this directly one autumn when he came to the Unity in Fort Worth, Texas. My first marriage had fallen apart and I was deeply depressed and worried about the effect it would have on my children. As I sat in the audience listening to his sermon, he suddenly seemed to falter slightly in his talk and look intently at me. Our eyes locked for a brief moment and then he moved on in his talk. At the end of the talk, Roy and the senior Unity minister were standing at the door, saying goodbye to the attendees. When I reached him, he reached out with his left hand, took my right hand and pulled me around to stand next to him. Still holding my hand, he continued saying goodbye to people as they filed past him. Seeing their looks, but not caring what they thought, holding tightly to his hand, not letting go, I slumped into him and put my head on his shoulder. I sighed, head down, and when I did, I felt what can be only described as "liquid electric love," pour out of his left hand and into my right. It flowed up my arm, across my shoulder, and into my heart. When it reached my heart, it was if an empty cup was being filled. I stood next to him struggling not to cry. When my heart was filled to overflowing, the pain and heartache seemed to subside and in its place was a gentle peace and acceptance. He continued to hold my hand as he said the last of his goodbyes. We then walked out to the parking lot silently, hand-in-hand. As we got to his car, he turned me around. Looking deep into my eyes, he said, "Stay out of your head." Smiling broadly, full of love, he hugged me, then he climbed into his car and waved goodbye.

I never told him what was going on during that year. He just seemed to know. His intuitive abilities were astounding, but he rarely, if ever, talked about them or his own internal spiritual experiences. Once, while on retreat, a woman relayed a piece of information to him that he didn't know. When she realized he hadn't known about it, she said, "Why Mr. Davis, I thought you knew everything." To which my Guru replied, "Madame, if I knew everything at the same time, I would be the most confused man on the planet."

Roy was relentlessly asked question everywhere he went. Some were sincere and heartfelt to which he always responded with appropriate and thoughtful concern, while others were intentionally rude, and still other questions were meant to bait him. Several times, over the years, I heard someone ask him, "Are you enlightened?" The question is a trap. If he said yes, he would be perceived as arrogant, and if he had said no, he would be deemed unworthy. But my Guru was too smart to fall into the trap and I heard him tactfully answer the question in several ways over the years. He once answered the question by saying, "I am no longer ever unaware of what I am." Another time I heard him respond by saying, "I am very awake and I awaken more every day." When I heard him say the last one, it had such a profound effect on my own psyche, I took it as my own personal affirmation. Each morning when I awaken, I say to myself, "I am very awake and I awaken more every day."

Roy was a relentless learner and a voracious reader. He had a lifelong love affair with books and magazines. His own personal library had hundreds of volumes of yoga books as well as New Thought, Buddhism, and other enlightenment traditions. When he traveled, he would buy several magazines to read on the plane. He read widely including subjects on natural science, physics, astrophysics, and health, to name a few. He once told us that the world opened up to him through books and the way he found his own Guru, Paramahansa Yogananda, was through a health magazine. He wrote over fifty books during his lifetime as well as dozens of courses, hundreds of booklets, and thousands of articles.

Roy was always well-informed and could easily converse on many topics, though he was reluctant to chat. But more than that, he was wise. His wisdom and discernment came from the profound depths of his realization and when I was in his presence, I was acutely aware of not only his intelligence, but his intimate, experiential relationship with the Divine. Spirit flowed through him and as him. When surrendered to God and in tune with him, my own awareness of God seemed magnified and my spiritual paradigm expanded beyond its previous boundaries. Often when I traveled to see him, I would arrive at CSA wearied by life, tired of the struggles with a negative outlook. But, after being in his presence for just a few hours, I would experience a consciousness shift, and life would once again seem bright with endless possibilities for positive outcomes.

Roy was a Sat Guru in the true sense of the word. He could enter the consciousness of a willing and prepared disciple and assist them in a shift of their consciousness paradigm. Over the years, I experienced Roy entering my consciousness and assisting me several times. Once, while again on retreat, I was meditating with him in the meditation hall when I suddenly found myself in a clear space of awareness. With eyes closed and raised, I began to experience what seemed like lightning with astral rain of many colors pouring down upon me. Om began to ring in my ears and a great bliss came over me, followed by a profound stillness. As the experience began to fade and I returned to ordinary consciousness, to myself I said, "Holy shit!" Just as I had that thought, I opened my eyes to find Roy intently staring at me and chuckling to himself. When our eyes met, he looked away, shoulders heaving trying to contain his laughter. It was obvious to me he knew exactly what I had experienced and inwardly had heard my expletive.

Only once, in the more than thirty years I knew him, did I block him from my mind. He had snapped at me about something. I don't remember what it was after all these years, but it hurt my feelings. Inwardly, I said "that's it, you can't come in anymore." With that, I closed him off from my thoughts. Not long after that, he came to Dallas, TX to give a seminar. I helped organize it, and attended the seminar. I was calm and attentive, but inwardly distant. Unbeknownst to me, he cornered my wife half-way through the seminar and said, "What's going on with Mike?" I hadn't told her that he had hurt my feelings and I had cut him off. So, she said, "I don't know what you're talking about, I only know he wants to be ordained." At the end of the seminar, Roy was getting into the car of a student who lived by the airport and was going to drive him to it on her way home. He stood by the open car door and said "Mike, come here." I walked over and he said to me, "Next time I come back to Dallas, I'm going to ordain you." He hugged me and got into the car. All was forgiven, and I never locked him out of my mind again.

Our consciousness is without boundaries. Our awareness has borders and restrictions; it's a bubble we live in with cognitive biases, subliminal activators, and subconscious habits and inclinations. The more awake we are, and the more we realize our true identity, the more we live in consciousness and the less we live in our restricted awareness bubbles. Roy's qualitative work was with his personal disciples, and he never failed to assist them in awakening to new and less restricted consciousness-paradigms if they were prepared and open to him helping them.

MICHAEL C. GADWAY

Chapter 5

The Dissolution of Ego

It's not in the doing, it's in the being. Let God whisper how to be

There is a philosophical and practical methodology integrated into all enlightenment traditions: the process of spiritual evolution and growth by the systematic dismantling of the ego, along with the attachments and aversions inherent to it. This is referred to as the transformation of consciousness, or the science of Self-realization. We often simply refer to it as the inner work. The ego, that false sense of a separate existence, is a result of our forgetting the truth of our being. With this forgetting comes a sense of an individualized awareness and, the Vedic philosophers say, suffering is the inevitable result. The practice of spirituality is less about going to a church to socialize, and more about the involution of awareness to realize the truth at our core. The ego, with its corresponding subliminal habits, patterns, and activators, often identifies with the contents of the mind, and our identification with it and those mental contents, prevents us from awakening to the truth of our being. Part of the Guru's role is to facilitate the dissolution of the ego, thereby assisting the spiritual student in their quest for the God and Self-realization.

Sometimes this comes in the form of love, and other times it comes in the form of discipline. Over the years I have heard people describe my Guru as "not squishy," "strict," or "emotionally distant." But that was not my experience. With me, Roy was loving and kind. He always greeted me with a hug and genuinely inquired about my well-being. Over the years he told me he loved me several times and I loved him dearly. A true Guru doesn't give the disciple what he or she wants. A true Guru gives them what they need.

Roy never shied away from disciplining his disciples if it was required, and I was no exception. I remember once, a spiritual friend of mine had hurt my feelings and I was righteously angry, or so I thought. He was at CSA for a retreat at the same time I was and when I saw him in the dining hall, I was cold, distant, and curt when we met. Roy was in the meditation hall, and when I saw him enter the room, I approached him to ask a personal question. Walking up to him, I expected to be greeted the way he always did, with a hug and a smile. But instead, he was cold, distant, and curt. I walked away from the encounter confused and as I walked away, it hit me. He was treating me the same way I had just treated my friend. I thought, I'm going to see if that was a coincidence or if Roy was teaching me a lesson. So, the next time I saw my friend, I was polite, but still distant. A few hours later, I saw Roy and sure enough, he was polite, but distant. The next time I saw my friend, I was open, relaxed, and cheerful. Again, walking up to Roy to ask him something, he hugged me, and was the kind and loving Guru I had come to expect.

Obviously, he had intuited what was going on and was teaching me how to practice loving-kindness, regardless of perceived hurts or malignments.

It is interesting to note that when disciples don't like their own personas, they will often put on the persona of their Guru, erroneously assuming it is the way spiritual authorities behave. I watched this occur with Roy's disciples many times through the years. Roy was genuinely quiet and observant. He was naturally shy and introverted. When in public he was reserved and always polite. But he was also approachable and kind. He was easy to talk to, and he was adept at the art of conversation when he needed to be. But when his disciples, especially his older ministers, tried to behave like him, it came off as cold and distant because it wasn't natural. When they tried to mimic his behavior, it appeared as an affectation and it was off-putting. Their behavior was just another side to the ego coin and not sincere.

Roy never told us we had to have his personality when we were ministering. He always advocated authenticity and encouraged us to be appropriate and Spirit-led at all times. He was not trying to produce automatons. My Guru knew the value of spiritual authenticity and always supported us in being true spiritual conduits through which Spirit could express fully. Yoga teaches us that we are all the same at the core. The subtlety of ego is when we separate ourselves by claiming to be special saying, "I am part of this organization or that religion," or "My teacher is greater than yours." Spirit will not be confined by ownership, but it will be shut out by hubris.

I remember having a private conversation with him during which I expressed my dislike of a certain personality trait I had. He looked at me and said, "Oh Mike, by the time you're my age you will know it's just personality, and you'll leave it behind."

Over the years I keenly observed Roy and the way he interacted with people. He always treated everyone as his equal. He never condescended or acted towards anyone with disrespect. But at the same time, he had no tolerance for arrogance or egotistical behavior, and he would shut it down quickly with either cool unresponsiveness or by ignoring it completely. I witnessed many people over the years come to CSA expecting preferential treatment, usually for their intellect or their money, or some other perceived specialness. They were met with simple indifference by my Guru. He was only interested in our spiritual growth and doing what he could to expediate that process. The people with delusions of grandeur usually left, dissatisfied and as quickly as they had arrived. Some even left angry that their expectations had not been met.

I also witnessed some amusing interactions between Roy and seminar attendees. While I was living in Texas, whenever Roy was speaking in churches or giving seminars in Texas, I would drive to see him. He came to Texas two or three times each year for nearly a decade, and I never missed one of his presentations. After the presentation, a line of attendees would usually form to talk with him. I never presumed preferential treatment, and I too would get in line. But, every time I would get to the front of the line and greet him, he would reach his left hand out, take my right hand, and steer me around to stand next to him on his left. Sometimes he would continue to hold my hand while talking with each attendee in turn. I just stood next to him, watching and listening. I always had the sense that he was training me in how to interact with people spiritually. After one of the seminars, he was approached by a small Indian man. Looking up to my tall Guru, he said, in a strong Indian accent, "Mr. Davis, what happens if I go into Nirvikalpa samadhi and can't get out?" Looking down, Roy responded, "Sir, if you go into Nirvikalpa samadhi, you won't care if you come out or not." Another time while standing next to him, a long line had formed of people waiting to talk with him. The line extended through the door and into the hallway. Patiently, Roy focused on each attendee in turn, politely answering their questions and making them feel seen and heard. I looked up to see a very large woman come through the door, pushing her way through the line. When she got about four feet away from Roy, she took a step to the side opened her arms wide and bellowed out for everyone to hear, "Roy, do you need a hug?" Roy looked up and said firmly, "No." Then he looked back to the person in line and picked up the conversation where they had left off. The woman's arms dropped to her sides and I watched as her face turned various shades of red. With a huff, she stormed out shoving people out of her way as she went. Caught off guard by the surrealism of the moment, I burst out laughing, which earned me a stern look from my Guru demanding I behave.

Egos are often rooted in deep seated feelings of unworthiness and I was no exception. The greatest lesson Roy taught me by way of ego dismantling happened without him even being aware of what had taken place. Often God will use an awakened Soul to assist his devotees towards enlightenment without that awakened Soul knowing it.

After my son died, it was five years before I could return to CSA. Silence can increase focus and the quiet solitude of being at CSA proved to be too much for me; it exacerbated my grief and I had to stay away. I stayed in touch with Roy through email and an occasional phone call, but it was four years before I saw him again. I had moved to Oregon to go to school and while there, Roy came to California for a conference. Being only a day's drive from Portland, my wife and I decided to drive down for the weekend and attend the seminar. The morning after we arrived, I went down to the breakfast room to get coffee. As I walked in, I saw Roy enjoying breakfast with his wife, Willie. At first, I was hesitant to interrupt them but I thought, "I'll just say a quick hello, then leave them alone." I walked up to their table and said, "Hi Roy, how are you?" Roy looked up from his meal and said "Fine," then looked back down at his food. Confused, I looked at Willie and said, "Hi Willie," she stared briefly at me, then with a look of surprise said, "Hi Mike." Roy looked back up at me in silence. Feeling out of place and as if I was bothering them, I said, "I just wanted to say hello. I'll see you later at the seminar." I walked away rattled by the interaction and not understanding what had just happened. As I got to the door, I realized, he had no idea who I was. I stopped dead in my tracks and thought, "Oh, I better process this immediately." I went and found a quiet corner next to the lobby to think. Sitting down in disbelief and saying to myself, "How is it possible after being his disciple for the last twenty years, he didn't recognize me? Did I mean so little to him that once I wasn't around anymore, he forgot all about me?" While pondering this, and feeling very sorry for myself, I suddenly had the thought, "Why did you come Michael? Did you come for praise and accolade? Does your ego need to be recognized and lauded over, or did you come for liberation?" With those thoughts, I made the decision to look at the situation as a spiritual growth opportunity, act like a grown up, and get on with it. I sighed deeply, stood up, stepped over my ego lying dead on the floor in front of me, and went up to the hotel room. As I opened the door, my wife came out of the bathroom to greet me. Still stinging from the ego bruise, I said to her, "Roy didn't recognize me." Confused, she said, "What?" I said, "I just saw him in the breakfast room and he had no idea who I was." She said, "Oh honey." She hugged me tightly. Then, held me at arm's length and looking deep in my eyes she said, "Honey... you're fat." I said, "What?" She said, "Baby, you've gained so much weight, I hardly recognize you." Hurt by her response I said, "That's rude." She shrugged and walked back into the bathroom. She was right though, after my son died, I had eaten my way through the grief and gained more than twenty pounds. I barely recognized myself in the mirror. How could

I expect Roy to recognize me? In his defense, later that day, I stood in line to get his autograph on an original copy of *Time, Space, and Circumstances*, and when I got to the front of the line, he did what he had always done. He reached across the table, took my right hand in his left hand and brought me around next to him. I kneeled down to be at the same height he was, and as he signed book after book, he made a moment that was special just for me.

Roy had a gift that few have. He could carve out a moment of profound spiritual awareness and share it with disciples in the midst of chaos and confusion. He would look at you and when you met his gaze, you could feel the transfer of spiritual energy at an inexplicably deep level; it was a moment of absolute stillness that transcended this mundane reality. My friend Daniel Bledsoe once shared an experience he had with Roy. He said he was sitting in the Meditation Hall during a retreat, and when Roy was done talking and had dismissed the room, Roy got up from his chair and looking deeply into my Daniel's eyes, he struck the gong. Daniel said that as Roy struck the gong and looked into his eyes, the kundalini surged up his spine so strongly he had to sit back and wait quietly before he could get up and go into the Dining Hall. As a Self-realized yoga master, my Guru had the ability to share this energy with a look, a touch, or a thought. Sometimes Spirit took over and shared the energy when he walked into the room even without Roy consciously transferring it.

Not every student could withstand the process of Self-transformation. Over the years I knew several disciples who left because the spiritual training was too hard for them, or as the Buddhists say, the "arrogance of enlightenment" falsely made them believe they no longer needed a Guru. Some have even gone so far as to claim they never had a Guru, and that they themselves are the Guru. I was astounded when some of Roy's disciples of nearly twenty years left him and when asked who their teacher was, they claimed they were self-taught and never had a Guru. In yogic terms, this is considered a grave error in judgment. Roy never discussed his disciples or their progress, or lack thereof, with anyone. I witnessed several reunions with Roy and a student who had obviously betrayed their sacred relationship. Roy always met them with open arms and a welcome smile. Only once, that I know of, did a previous disciple ask to return to the fold and Roy told them no. Roy's response to that student was that it would be better for them to be on their own.

With a true Sat Guru, there is an integrated process of support and encouragement while ego and arrogance are being dissolved. This process can sometimes lead to challenges as the restrictions of the mind are weeded out, and the awakening of Soul awareness is nurtured. But it is a requirement that the mind must be cleansed for Spirit to express fully. Patanjali's Yoga Sutras states that when the mind is as pure as the Soul, Illumination dawns. To be accepted as a disciple of Roy Eugene Davis was to enter this process of awakening, and I am not exaggerating when I tell you, this took a great deal of inner fortitude. But if his disciples remained faithful and forged ahead, the worthwhile results were a humility, strength, and spiritual awakening that no one could take from us. Roy revealed the truth. He never wavered, and he never grew weary of supporting us in our quest for liberation.

Chapter 6

The Patterns of Our Lives
Once again, I take my seat and fingers dance, to weave the kismet throw of hap and chance

The spiritual path is not for the faint of heart. When Roy first formally talked with Paramahansa Yogananda in 1949, Yoganandaji said to him, "This is not the path of escapism you know." To which my Guru responded, "I know sir."

Through the years, I heard many people ask Roy the same question over and over again. "Do I have to experience my karma?" This was not a question asked from intellectual curiosity; it was a question anchored in fear. What they were really asking was, "I am afraid to experience the consequences of my past choices and actions, must I?"

MICHAEL C. GADWAY

While at CSA one summer, an older female disciple of Roy's asked me that same question to which I responded, "All karma must be faced." Vehemently disagreeing, she indignantly said, "Well, I'm just going to ask Roy." I nodded and remained quiet as her anger caught me off guard. She marched into the meditation hall and sat down armed with her righteous indignation and determined to get Roy to agree with her. When she asked him the question, his response was measured and carefully diplomatic. He talked about how karma can be overcome and we are not victims of fate. We have a say in how we respond to what is presented to us as we are spiritual beings superior to the body and the mind. But he never directly responded to her question with a yes or no answer. After the session, believing she held the philosophical high ground, she strode up to me and said, "See, I told you we didn't have to experience our karma." I remained steadfastly silent. But Roy never said that. She was so hungry to be validated and hear what she wanted to hear; she hadn't actually listened to his answer. I heard from friends over the years that sadly, her life became very difficult with many challenges, and she eventually stopped coming to CSA and connecting with Roy.

Yoga does not teach us we can escape karma and pain. It teaches us we can rise above karma and suffering. Pain and suffering are not the same. The Vedic concept of suffering is very different from the Westerner's understanding. The word in Sanskrit is Dukham. It literally means, 'Bad axle hole.' It is the understanding that suffering is a function of the mind. When we are presented with challenging patterns and circumstances, the mind goes looking for the answers. Most often, when we come to the answer, we resist the choice we need to make to resolve it. The mind moves on past the answer not accepting the resolution presented to it, and returns to its starting point. Suffering in the Vedic sense is more akin to emotional angst; the mind goes around and around refusing the resolution and therefore the dissolution of the karma. According to the Vedas, this can go on for lifetimes as it is the individualized mind and its contents the Soul takes with it from incarnation to incarnation. The truth is the freedom we so desperately desire waits for us down the path we most vehemently resist.

On another occasion, while Roy was answering that same question about karma, he suddenly looked at me intently and said, "You know there's a reason they say those who are closest to the fire most often get burnt." A shudder ran up my spine. Then, his demeanor softened and still looking at me he said, "But it will be okay." Then he turned away and continued talking. I went home at the end of the week and four days later, I was caught in a grease fire and suffered second and third degree burns over forty percent of my right arm. The grease also dripped onto my right foot, burning two holes halfway through it. I ended up in the burn victim unit of Parkland Hospital in Dallas, Tx. But just as my Guru had predicted, after months of uncomfortable rehabilitation, I was okay. I believe, though I have no objective evidence, that it could have been much worse. Just before the fire ignited, I was suddenly surrounded with my Guru's presence and a great stillness overcame me. I knew something inevitable was about to happen and a surrendered peace filled me. After the burning, I calmly called the ambulance and began to run my arm under cool water. The pain was overwhelming, yet I remained in that calm place. I never discussed it with him and he never asked.

So many times over the years, I was aware of Roy spiritually intervening on my behalf, yet he never talked about it or hinted that he had helped me. He was selfless and humble and most people were completely unaware of his abilities to mediate between the Soul and God.

Calling Roy and describing a difficult personal experience I was going through, he said. "Sometimes Mike, all we can do is ride the wave."

Yet another time when I called him about a very difficult pattern in my life I was again experiencing, his response was, "You're not the problem are you?" Angrily I said, "No I'm not the problem." To which he said, "Okay, then you have to deal with the problem maturely." In other words, this was a pattern in my life and it was up to me to resolve it in order to dissolve it. Yet another time, during a retreat, he talked about how it was possible to recognize mental patterns and challenges, and take them into superconscious meditation and dissolve the very idea of them. In other words, take the idea of the challenge into the causal and dissolve it at the seed. He said, "You just see the nothingness of it." At the time I couldn't grasp what he meant by that. But the next summer when I came for retreat, I was being challenged by a negative pattern in my mind. When I sat to meditate with him, I felt his consciousness in my mind and I was suddenly lifted up into a superconscious state. There, looking at the problem, I realized the "nothingness of it," and inwardly saw the very idea of it dissolve. That problem never bothered me again.

However, each situation is an individualized experience. On several occasions, I listened as students asked Roy the same question. He answered differently every time. My Guru could read the inner conditions of his students and he tailored his answers specifically, in a way that helped the student the most. Unfortunately, the simple minded often universalized his advice and would share that same advice in inappropriate ways and at inappropriate times, not realizing the advice was for them alone.

One of the surprising side effects of going to CSA and being in Roy's presence for a prolonged period of time was that I often became very ill while I was there. Throughout my life, I have rarely been sick or needed medical assistance. I can honestly say that over my lifetime, I have seen a doctor only a handful of times and most of those were for health checkups. But for some reason when I stayed at CSA, I would often get sick. On one such occasion, I went to the meditation hall to hear him speak, keeping a safe distance from the other retreat participants. Looking directly at me during his talk he said, "Often when spiritual aspirants come here, the energy triggers various releases in both the body and the mind. If we stay calm and centered, they will work themselves out naturally."

Some karma must be experienced, some karma must be resolved, and yet other karma, we simply take into super consciousness and dissolve it. But all karma must be faced. I am often confused by people resisting the idea of facing their karma. The truth is, we are living our karma; this is it. How do we know what karma is ours? What is in front of us is ours to face. There is no running from it or avoiding it. In the Bhagavad Gita, when Arjuna tells Krishna he will not face his Karma, Krishna, the enlightened Soul, tells him to stop embarrassing himself, to stand up and be the spiritual warrior he was born to be. It is the same for us all. This may seem to be a cold response to a hard world but, I think rather, it is a realistic response to a spiritual law.

Judgmentally, we often refer to "good" karma, and "bad" karma, depending on whether or not what we are experiencing is perceived as causing mental affliction or not. But karma is neither good or bad, black or white, inevitable or escapable; it is simply the expression of past actions or mental patterns coming to fruition. It is up to us to learn to respond with emotional clarity and maturity, knowing that what in front of us is temporary. After all, everything with a beginning must have an end.

MICHAEL C. GADWAY

Chapter 7

In This World and the Next

When clarion calls aloud and home I am returned, Though none may see that I have gone, in God's embrace I am interred

Heartache and sorrow are part of this dream play we call life and spiritual aspirants are not insulated from the darkness and the demons because we strive towards the light. To all of us come troubles, challenges, and sufferings. To be born in this world is to know loss and pain. I have never met a human being who has not suffered in some way and every saintly person I have ever come in contact with has been on intimate terms with suffering; if they had not suffered, they could not help us free ourselves from our own suffering. Their advice would be intellectual pulp without truth, meaning, substance, and experience behind it.

Suffering comes in many forms, but one of the most devastating ways is when we lose a loved one in an untimely manner. I was forty-four when my sixteen-year-old son David was hit by a truck on his bicycle and killed. When I called Roy, obviously devasted, his response was genuine and caring. He said, "Oh Mike, that's awful. I'm so sorry." Then he said, "What can I do?" I said, "Would you pray for us?" Roy seemed surprised by this simple request and said, "I can do that!" I think people often asked him for impossible miracles. But I knew destiny had played her cards and the only path forward was through the grief process and eventually acceptance.

During the more than thirty years I was with Roy, there was never a significant event that I did not include him in either through a letter, email, or phone call. Inwardly I kept him close in consciousness and his spirit was always with me. But his presence and strength were especially evident when life became very difficult.

Ten years after my son's death, my wife was diagnosed with pancreatic cancer. We had just retired and were looking forward to spending the rest of our lives in quiet togetherness. I was going to write and perhaps teach a little and she was going to pursue art therapy which she had always loved. Just seven weeks after her diagnosis, she was gone and I was left to face the world alone.

While she was dying, I chose to make her final days sacred. Our house was open to her friends and family, and many people came to pray and meditate with us. We would chant the names of God in Sanskrit and hold prayer vigils through the day. I brought in a sound-light therapist and she filled our home with beautiful music and sound. Our home became a spiritual pilgrimage for many of those who knew my wife. They would come just to sit by her and spend time in her presence. Many who came experienced emotional and spiritual healing.

During her illness, I brought in a hospital bed and set it up in the master bedroom for her. But it was too small for me to sleep with her so, I put a pallet on the floor next to her bed to sleep. She was confusing her days and her nights and she would get up in the middle of the night disoriented. I was worried she would fall, so I was always there with her. During those last weeks I averaged three to four hours of sleep a night and worked all day taking care of her.

It was during these last weeks that I had a powerful astral experience with my Guru. Sleeping on the pallet, I became aware of myself in astral form sitting in lotus posture on the floor of a small astral hall. The hall was pure white with a tall vaulted ceiling. There at the front of the hall, on a raised dais, was my Guru meditating in lotus posture. He opened his eyes, and when he looked down and saw me, he seemed surprised I was there. I turned my head, looking to my left, and saw several other men meditating with him, also sitting in lotus posture along the wall. When I looked back at Roy, he was standing in front of me. I looked up and he bent down putting his forehead on my forehead and a great light broke upon me. In my grief and pain, I cried out. When I did, I was drawn back into the body where it lay on the floor. With my eyes still closed, crying softly, I felt a great pressure in the Guru chakra and looking deeply into it, my Guru's voiced echoed through my mind, "Take refuge in me!"

It is said when a devotee of this Guru lineage passes, one of the Gurus is there to help the disciple into the next realm. I can verify this as fact from my own experience. I intuitively knew when my wife approached her last hours. Sitting next to her, I meditated while she lay dying. Realizing it was time for her to leave, I put my left hand over her heart and my right hand over her forehead. Looking deeply into the third eye hoping to make final contact with her, I heard Roy's voice in my head. "Go for a walk." Not wanting to leave I answered aloud, "I want to stay." He again spoke to me, but this time it was a command, "Go for a walk!" Whispering a prayer and inwardly saying goodbye to her, I got up and went outside. I sat on the sidewalk for several minutes as she passed from this world into the next.

The Autumn Truth Journal magazine announced her passing later that year. The interesting part of the announcement is that it described who was sitting in the room with her when she passed. Roy and I never discussed who was in the room. He knew because he was there.

I am sometimes asked, "What do you think Roy is doing now?" I can answer with certainty. He is working with advanced disciples in the astral realm, assisting them towards liberation just as he did when he was here in the material realm.

Chapter 8

The Last Years and Final Goodbye

I sometimes ask myself, "When the seasons of my life have all run out, and I stand at the window looking at the snow blanketed forest, shimmering white in the last days of my winter, will I be able to say, well-met, well-lived, well-ended?"

Roy and I never discussed the future and I don't know what he knew. He always kept his own counsel. But there were several times, over the years, he hinted at a possible spiritual future for me. I have always avoided organizations and organizational work: preferring to rely on my own abilities rather than relying on others. I never wanted to be responsible for any organization, and I was averse to socializing. I'm not shy, but I am introverted, and it is why, even though I was a minister for CSA and Roy's disciple, I never started my own ministry.

When I was forty-two, Roy looked at me one day and said, "Isn't it time for you to retire?" Nonplussed by his question, I said, "Roy, I'm only forty-two!" He said, "Oh..." and then, "Mike wouldn't it be great if we could train professional CSA ministers?" Not understanding what he was getting at, I said, "Sure." Over the next fifteen years, every now and then, he would stop in the middle of our conversations and say those same words to me. "Isn't it time for you to retire?" and then "Wouldn't it be great if we could train professional CSA ministers?"

The year after my wife died, I came to CSA for a summer retreat. As you can imagine, my life had been turned upside down and overnight, my future plans had been wiped away. In my head, I had been praying for several weeks, "God, please find me a reason to wake up in the morning, a purpose and a mission. Please God, find me a way to serve." While there, one day, Roy suddenly looked at me and said, "You know Mike, when I was with Master, he would often say, 'You have a wonderful future Roy.' But he never told me what that future was. So, the Gurus have plans for you, be patient. Maybe the timing is just not right yet." At that point, the last thing I wanted to be was patient. But his words proved prophetic and there has been opportunity to serve.

For the last five years of Roy's life, I made a decision that when I was with him, I would behave as the old Guru-disciple tradition dictated. I would not approach him with questions, I would wait for him to acknowledge me and then, if he wanted to talk about something, I would enter the conversation. I did this for two reasons: the first being, at that point in my life, I didn't have many questions either philosophically or practically, and if I did, he always seemed to answer them during his talks. The second was, when I was in his presence, I was nearly always meditating with eyes open. I wanted to be receptive to his consciousness and I didn't want words to get in the way. But in the summer of 2018, while visiting him at CSA, during meditation, I heard an inner voice say, "If you want to talk to him, you need to ask him. Your ego is getting in the way." So, the next day, after the morning session, I got up from my chair and began to walk to the front of the meditation hall to ask if I could talk to him. I watched as he started to get out of his chair. He suddenly said, "Oh!" and sat back down. I walked up to him and asked if I could talk to him privately that week. Not saying anything, he looked far away. Mistaking his silence for rejection, my thought was, "Oh, he doesn't want to see me, he's just too polite to say no." Roy didn't realize that I hadn't said it out loud when he answered me, "No, I'm just thinking of a good time for us to meet." We set an appointment for Friday morning and I walked away glad that I was going to get to spend time alone with him.

Early on in my discipleship, during one of my retreat visits, the energy was so strong that I couldn't sleep one night. Finally giving up, I got up and went to the library. I read for a while, meditated for a time, and finally about 3am, I fell asleep on the floor behind one of the book cases. Later in the morning, I passed Roy on the sidewalk. He smiled broadly at me and said, "Sleep, okay?" I smiled back at him knowing he knew exactly how my night had gone. Later that afternoon, during class, Roy talked about how the spiritual energy at CSA can affect us. During his talk, smiling, he looked at me and said, "So don't go getting goofy on me." From then on, whenever I was going to spend time with him, I would pray to God on my way to our meeting, "Please Lord, don't let me be goofy."

MICHAEL C. GADWAY

Walking up the road to his chalet for our meeting, my head was down, praying "Please Lord don't let me be goofy." As I climbed the hill and rounded the corner, looking up, I saw Roy standing on the porch of his chalet. He smiled at me and opened his arms wide by way of greeting. My heart jumped for joy looking forward to being with him. We sat down together, he in his chair, and me on the couch. We spent more than two hours in conversation, sharing our love of books and discussing a broad range of topics. I didn't care what we talked about; I was just glad to spend time with him. While we were talking about the books, he said, "Where is your book? What is taking so long?" Earlier that year I sent him the manuscript for Ashtanga Yoga, and asked him for editorial comments. He sent me back several edits with his approval. But I was having trouble deciding on the cover. When I told him this, he said, "When we're done, we'll go down to the office and look at covers."

The conversation was pleasant and relaxed, He did most of the talking and I was content to listen and be in his presence. At one point he told me a funny story about an interaction he had with Yoganandaji. I had never heard the story, and as far as I know he had never shared it before. Leaning towards me, just a few inches from my face, he delivered the punch line with perfect timing. I burst out laughing with tears pouring from my eyes. Roy sat back in his chair with a self-satisfied smile at having rendered me incapacitated with laughter. Suddenly his mood changed, and he became somber. He said, "You know, that first year I was with Master, a great light seemed to come from him. But that last year, the light seemed to dim." Then he looked at me with a look I had never seen before. But if he was telling me something, I missed it. He looked healthier than I had seen him look in several years. I said, "Don't you think he worked himself to death?" Looking disappointed, Roy only nodded. Less than a year later, he was gone. Some have said Roy didn't know he was leaving, he knew. It is not possible for someone as awake as he was to not know. But true to his persona, he never directly told anyone. He was a man of quiet dignity and reserved expression. He was averse to drama and theatrics.

It had been nearly two years since my wife had died and I felt healed enough to begin again. I was looking for opportunities to interact with the world when I said to him, "I'm ready now to represent you and CSA." Roy began to nod yes then stopped, he seemed to be looking far off into the future for a moment. Then he looked at me intensely and said firmly, "And this Kriya Yoga tradition." His look was so intense I could only nod, unable to voice my agreement. His direct statement felt more like a mandate than an afterthought. I took what he said to heart and inwardly committed to represent him and this Kriya Yoga lineage if the opportunity ever presented itself.

We sat together in his chalet talking and enjoying each other's company. He made tea. I forgot to drink it. When we were done, he invited me to lunch with him and the staff in the office building. But I had lunch plans and had to decline. As we walked out of his chalet on that last visit he said, "Mike, wouldn't it be great if we could train professional CSA ministers?" It wasn't until a few years after he passed that it dawned on me, he might have been telling me something. I've always been slow that way.

We drove down to the office building and went inside. We spent time looking at his book covers and he explained the process and cost to me. When we were done, he hugged me goodbye. As I left, I turned back to see him standing, looking at me. He stood tall and strong, and he seemed to glow with pride. Love shone from his face; I felt that love and carry it with me to this day. It was the last time I saw him in the body.

For three days the following March, a black astral cloud hovered in the air. I felt a deep and inescapable sense of sadness. On the third day I received an email that my Guru had passed. I was saddened and introspective, but I wasn't surprised. My awareness of his presence and consciousness has not dimmed since his passing. Each morning before meditation, I acknowledge and honor my Guru before I turn the searchlight of my attention inward. Often, I am acutely aware of his spirit ever guiding me toward to Source. His spiritual influence is felt as strong today as it ever was, and I am continually grateful.

I once asked him, "Do you ever feel the weight of your responsibility as spiritual leader and Guru. He said, "No, I have always known I am not the doer. God is the only doer." I keep his words in in my heart and on the forefront of my mind as I move through my days. These words have become especially relevant since his passing. There have been many challenges to face and staunch, even vitriolic resistance to overcome. His love and spiritual training have been invaluable. So many opportunities for growth and actualization have come my way since his passing. Always his spirit and consciousness guide me. Someday I will stand in front of him and say, "I did my best to represent you and CSA, and this Kriya Yoga tradition."

www.ingramcontent.com/pod-product-compliance
Lightning Source LLC
Chambersburg PA
CBHW060857050426
42453CB00008B/991